# NATURAL WORLD

# TIGER

## HABITATS • LIFE CYCLES • FOOD CHAINS • THREATS

# Valmik Thapar

RSVP

RAINTREE
STECK-VAUGHN
PUBLISHERS
A Steck-Vaughn Company

Austin, Texas

# NATURAL WORLD

## Chimpanzee • Elephant • Giant Panda • Great White Shark
## Killer Whale • Lion • Polar Bear • Tiger

**Cover:** Face-to-face with a large male tiger
**Title page:** A tiger resting in the heat of day.
**Contents page:** An aggressive female approaches the photographer.
**Index page:** A tiger in its prime

Published by Raintree Steck-Vaughn Publishers, an imprint of Steck-Vaughn Company

**Library of Congress Cataloging-in-Publication Data**
Thapar, Valmik.
    Tiger / Valmik Thapar.
        p.    cm.—(Natural world)
    Includes bibliographical references and index.
    Summary: Explains the physical characteristics, life cycle, habits, habitat, and endangered status of the tiger.
    ISBN 0-7398-1055-3 (hard)
    0-7398-0946-6 (soft)
    1. Tigers—Juvenile literature.
    [1. Tigers.  2. Endangered species.]
    I. Title.  II. Series.
    QL737.C23T46   1999
    599.756—dc21                          98-53279

Printed in Italy. Bound in the United States.
1 2 3 4 5 6 7 8 9 0 04 03 02 01 00

**Picture acknowledgments**
All photographs by Fateh Singh Rathore and Valmik Thapar except: Clive Boursnell/BBC Wildlife Magazine *back cover*; Bruce Coleman Ltd 29 (Michael McKavett), 34 (Staffan Widstrand), 36 (Staffan Widstrand), 39 (Michael P Price), 45 bottom (Staffan Widstrand); David Lawson/WWF UK 41; Stockmarket 7; Tony Stone Images *front cover* (Art Wolfe), 11 (Chris Baker), 32 (Art Wolfe), 48 (James Balog); Joanna Van Gruisen 9.  Artwork by Michael Posen.

**Author's dedication**
For my nephew Jaisal Singh, and to Hannah, India, Stefano, Amina, Sonali, Amba, Sukanya, Vivaswath, Viveka, Abhinava, Radhika, Nikhil, Saurabh, Mrinal, Deeksha, Diva, Yuvraj, Prithvi, Surya, and so many others on whose shoulders will lie the future fate of the tiger and the natural treasures of this planet.

# Contents

Meet the Tiger  4

A Tiger Is Born  8

Growing Up  12

Learning to Hunt  20

Leaving Home  30

Threats  38

Tiger Life Cycle  44

Glossary  46

Further Information  47

Index  48

# Meet the Tiger

The tiger is one of the world's most powerful hunters. It is also one of the most secretive and is rarely seen in the wild. The tiger's striped coat is excellent camouflage among the shadows of the forest. It allows the tiger to slip through the forest almost unseen.

**Coat**
The Bengal tiger's coat blends in with the shadows of its habitat—forest and marshy grasslands. It helps the tiger stalk its prey without being seen.

**Tail**
A tiger's tail can be up to one-third of its total body length.

**Claws**
The claws are ideal for gripping and tearing flesh. They are normally held up inside the paws and flash out only when needed.

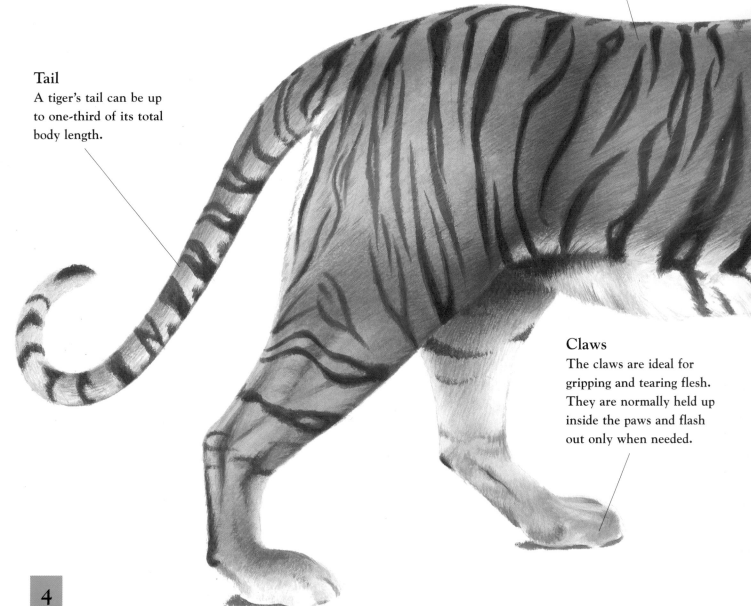

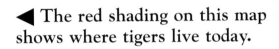

◀ The red shading on this map shows where tigers live today.

▼ A Bengal tiger bares its teeth.

**Ears**
Tigers have excellent hearing.

**Eyes**
The tiger's sharp eyes can detect the slightest movement even at night.

**Teeth**
The tiger's razor-sharp teeth are specially designed for tearing meat off the bone.

## TIGER FACTS

The tiger's Latin name is *Panthera tigris.*

●

Male Bengal tigers can grow to 12 ft. (3.5 m), including the tail, and can weigh up to 440 lbs. (200 kg). Females are smaller: up to about 8.5 ft. (2.6 m) and 350 lbs. (160 kg).

●

Tigers purr just like domestic cats, but the sound is about a hundred times louder.

## The World's Tigers

Until recently there were eight subspecies of tigers, but today only five are left. The Caspian tiger, once found in northern Iran, became extinct in the 1950s.

The Javan and Bali tigers, which lived on the islands of Java and Bali in Indonesia, are also extinct. Sumatra is now the only Indonesian island where tigers live, and there are only about 400 to 600 Sumatran tigers left.

▼ Tigers like water, and they are good swimmers. This Sumatran tiger is keeping itself cool.

▲ Siberian tigers have thick, furry coats to keep out the cold in Siberia.

There are about 1,500 to 1,800 Indo-Chinese tigers. The Chinese or South China tiger was once plentiful in parts of China, but today there are only 30 to 40 left. The largest tiger is the Siberian tiger. There are now about 400 Siberian tigers left.

The Indian or Bengal tiger lives in India, Nepal, Bhutan, Bangladesh, and possibly parts of Burma (Myanmar). They can live over 13,000 ft. (4,000 m) up in the mountains of Bhutan or at the edge of the sea in the mangrove swamps of the Sundarbans in India. There are about 3,000 to 4,000 alive today. This book will tell you about the life cycle of the Bengal tiger.

# A Tiger Is Born

It has been nearly 100 days since the tigress mated with the big male tiger that rules the area. The time has come for her to give birth.

First, she looks for a safe, secure den. When tiger cubs are very small, they can be killed by eagles or jackals, so they must be protected from any danger that might approach, either from the sky or on the ground.

▶ This tigress has made her den in a cave.

▼ A tigress will always make sure that her den is near water and in an area with plenty of animals to hunt.

8

When the cubs are born, the mother licks their fur with her rough tongue to help the blood flow around their bodies. In the first few weeks after giving birth, she devotes all her time to her cubs. Occasionally she rushes out to feed herself, but she always hunts near the den in case her cubs are threatened.

Usually only two or three cubs survive the first month. The tigress spends most of her time suckling them with her milk. As their eyes open, the cubs become very playful.

## TIGER CUBS

A tigress normally gives birth to two or three cubs, but there can be as many as six or seven. Newborn cubs normally weigh 2 to 3 lbs. (0.9–1.4 kg) and measure 9 to 15 in. (22–39 cm) long.

•

When the cubs are born, their eyes are closed and they are helpless. Their eyes may open in three days, or they may take up to two weeks.

◀ This two-week-old cub seeks shelter in its den, which is inside a thick bush.

The tigress attacks and chases away any intruder she finds. If she is disturbed too often, she will move the cubs, one by one, to a new den. She carries the cubs in her mouth, holding them gently by the scruff of the neck with her teeth.

In the second month, the tigress starts to teach the cubs to pay attention to her. She gives them an occasional slap with her paw or growls to make sure they obey her.

▼ A tigress with her one-month-old cub

# Growing Up

When the cubs are nearly two months old, the tigress starts bringing them parts of what she kills. She hunts farther away from the den now and may bring back food from more than a mile (1.6 km) away. The mother watches as the cubs nibble clumsily at the meat. Gradually, they stop drinking milk until their diet is nearly all meat.

The cubs grow quickly as they eat more meat. At about three or four months, their mother takes them for short walks around the den so that they can learn the sights and sounds.

▼ This tigress has killed a deer. She is carrying it back to her den to feed her cubs.

Once or twice a month the cubs' father will visit. He may have two or three families in his territory, and he tracks each of them down by the tigresses' scents, which they leave by spraying bushes and trees with their urine. When the male visits, the entire group may spend a day feasting over a kill before he moves on to see another of his families.

▲ The cubs' father (in the foreground) has come to visit the cubs and their mother.

## Exploring

As the cubs enter their fifth month, they walk longer distances with their mother, learning more about their world. The tigress teaches them about the ways of the forest and the other animals that live there.

Sometimes the cubs disturb the tigress while she is hunting. But at other times they may help her by flushing out small animals from the bush for her to pounce on. The cubs are now fully weaned. They stalk partridges and peacocks. They also leap after squirrels and hares. This is a time full of play.

▼ A tigress with her five-month-old cubs

14

▲ As the cubs grow, one of them becomes dominant.

The cubs grow quickly. They are always hungry, and the tigress has to hunt almost all the time to keep them fed. Gradually, one of the cubs grows more confident and becomes the leader of its brothers and sisters. This dominant cub is always the first to snatch the food the tigress catches. It quickly grows bigger than the other cubs.

By the seventh month, the cubs go almost everywhere with their mother. For their own safety, she has to keep the cubs quiet. She controls them by using various snarls, and sometimes she slaps them with her paw. One of the strangest noises the tigress makes sounds like a bird's peeping. This noise is enough to make the cubs hide right away.

▲ Two seven-month-old cubs follow their mother.

▼ A female tiger (on the left) fights off a male to protect her cubs.

Hunting is never easy. The tigress makes a kill only once in every fifteen attempts. While she hunts she must also watch out for bears, leopards, hyenas, and jackals that could be a threat to her cubs. Unknown tigers are also a danger, and the tigress must keep her young safe.

## TIGER PLAY

When they are young, cubs like climbing trees. They even jump and swing across the branches. After they are about sixteen months old, the cubs become too heavy for the branches to support their weight.

●

Tigers love water. Young cubs play games in the water and splash each other.

▲ A tigress watches a sambar deer in the water, waiting for her chance to pounce.

◀ Two young cubs play in a tree.

## Playing Games

By nine months old, the cubs have grown to about 6 ft. (1.8 m) from head to tail and weigh about 80 to 100 lbs. (36 to 45 kg). They play hide and seek, rush back and forth, box each other, race up trees and over rocks, and splash and jump in water. As well as having a great time, they are testing and strengthening their legs, which will be the most powerful parts of their bodies.

The tigress spends most of her time hunting. Her cubs are old enough to look after themselves, and she can travel several miles in a night while they stay near the den. When she returns after many hours away, the mother and her cubs greet each other with cuddles, licks, and hugs, and the sound of their purring fills the forest.

# Learning to Hunt

Over the next year, the cubs will learn how to hunt. They have already stalked birds and squirrels and chased crows and vultures away from their food. Now the serious training begins.

The tigress walks the cubs around her territory to teach them its secrets. She takes them to every lake and waterhole, to show them where deer and other prey gather to drink. In the wet season, when the deer move to higher ground, the tigers will follow them.

▼ Two cubs at the edge of a lake

▲ When she makes a kill, the mother tiger makes sure that all her cubs get a share of the food.

Sometimes the tigress will catch and injure a young animal without killing it. She will then watch from a distance to see how well her cubs kill and eat the animal.

Gradually, through many clumsy attempts, the young ones learn the skills of hunting. By twelve to fourteen months old, the cubs probably know how to kill peacocks and hares. They also stalk and chase young deer and antelope, young monkeys, and even wild boar piglets.

21

## How Tigers Hunt

Tigers prefer to hunt at dusk, at dawn, or in the dark of the night. This is when they can slip into the open like shadows and approach their prey in very dim light. Unlike some other big cats, a tiger does not chase its prey. Instead it stalks it carefully, creeping closer, step by step.

▼ A tiger attacks a deer in the shallow water of a lake.

## TIGER FOOD

Tigers hunt a wide range of animals—almost anything from birds such as peacocks to young rhinos and elephants. They also prey on snakes and young crocodiles. Near the sea, tigers even catch fish and crabs. Tigers also eat grass and mud that help them digest their food. A tigress with two or three cubs will kill up to 100 deer each year.

▼ Tigers are at the top of their food chain. Here are just a few of the animals that tigers hunt. (The illustration is not to scale.)

Porcupine

Sloth bear

Peacock

Buffalo

Sambar deer

When the tiger has crept to within a few yards of its prey, it pounces with a burst of speed on the animal. When it catches a deer, for example, it first uses the power of its front paw to smash into the animal, forcing it to tumble down. Its sharp canine teeth move in a flash to the deer's throat, to break the animal's neck or choke it to death.

## Staying Out of Sight

The cubs learn to recognize every sound and sight and how the other creatures of the forest react to their presence. Once the tiger's stripes are seen, the forest rings with the frightened calls of animals and birds—the sharp bark of the monkey, the booming alarm of the sambar deer, and the shriek of the peacock. These calls pinpoint the tiger's position and warn other creatures to keep away.

So, the cubs must learn to tread softly and silently, to stay in the cover provided by grasses, bushes, and trees and to stalk and move in slow motion to get close to their prey.

▶ A tiger lies in wait for prey. Its stripes help it to stay hidden in the long grass.

▼ This deer has seen the tiger and has a chance to escape.

◀ From high in the trees, this female monkey with her baby can keep watch for danger.

## The Tiger's Prey
In the forest, monkeys and deer keep close together to help protect each other from tigers. From their treetop perches, monkeys can see a tiger's stripes from a long way off. Deer have excellent hearing and a keen sense of smell. Whichever animal senses the tiger first warns the other.

▼ Wild buffaloes can kill tigers with their horns. But an adult tiger can usually kill a buffalo.

Monkeys also help provide food for the deer. As they feed in the trees, they knock down leaves and fruit, which are gobbled up greedily by the deer.

## Avoiding Danger

As well as learning which animals to hunt, young tigers must also find out which are dangerous and best to avoid. Tigers will hunt porcupines, but they have to be very careful. A porcupine's quills can stick in a tiger's paw or around its mouth. These painful wounds can become infected, and young tigers sometimes die because of this.

Much of the land where tigers live is shared by elephants. Tigers normally keep away from them, but they have been known to attack and kill young elephant calves.

▼ Tigers usually avoid rhinos, but they will attack young ones.

▲ Most tigers avoid sloth bears. Even so, big male tigers have been known to kill and eat these bears.

Tigers keep away from packs of wild dogs, but they may attack a small pack and steal its food. Tigers may also scavenge food from crocodiles in lakes and rivers, racing into the water and snatching the carcass away.

As they grow up, tigers also become wary of one another. When they are about sixteen months old, the cubs start to keep a little distance from each other. Their play becomes aggressive, and they swat, jump, and snarl at each other. This is a time when their lives change forever.

# Leaving Home

It is almost time for the cubs to begin leaving home. The mother knows this, and she starts to keep away from her largest cubs for a day or two. The dominant cub, which is nearly as big as its mother, has learned to attack and eat small animals and is the first to move away. At about eighteen months old, its canine teeth are fully formed.

The other cubs may stay for a few more months, depending on their hunting skills. While the cubs are getting ready to leave, the mother makes sure they have enough food.

▲ These cubs are twenty months old. Soon they will leave home.

▶ After leaving home, tigers live on their own most of the time.

## TIGER TERRITORY

In India, a tigress's territory might cover several square miles. A male tiger may have a territory of up to 116 sq. mi. (300 sq. km).

●

In Siberia, where the tigers' prey may be spread out over a wide area, the territory can stretch to 300 sq. mi. (800 sq. km).

By the time they are twenty-four months old, all the cubs have left. For the next twelve to sixteen months, the female cubs live in small parts of their mother's territory, but they keep out of their mother's way. They try to enlarge their territories—especially in areas where there are plenty of deer.

## Struggling to Survive

After they have left home, the male cubs stay in their mother's territory for over a year or find a refuge on the edges of another tiger's territory. They try to grow stronger and keep out of the way of other male tigers—including their father.

▼ Male tigers are often aggressive toward other males.

▲ A twenty-month-old cub cleans its paw.

This is a difficult time for all the cubs. They have to put their mother's training into practice and try to survive. Not all of them succeed.

Much of a tiger's time is spent resting, saving its energy for the hunt. Most of the hot day is spent sleeping in the shade or cooling off in a pool of water.

While tigers rest they groom themselves to keep clean. They use their tongues to lick and wash every part of their bodies, especially between their claws. A tiger's saliva is a strong antiseptic that heals small cuts and wounds caused by thorns or received while hunting.

## Fighting Each Other

Young tigers may fight each other for a mate or for new territory, especially the males, who can be very aggressive. The strongest, most aggressive tigers win control of the best territories, where there is the most food. The next-strongest tigers win the next-best territories.

▼ Once they have left home, the young tigers live on their own and rarely meet again.

Tigers sometimes meet when one has made a kill. Then there is much snarling and roaring, and they may have a ferocious tug-of-war over the carcass. The winner will then eat while the loser backs off and waits its turn.

In meetings like these, tigers test each other's strength. They stand up on their hind legs, snarling and boxing at each other until one of them submits by rolling over onto its back.

▲ When two tigers meet, they may fight until the weaker one gives in.

◀ This adult tigress is roaring to attract a male. The sound can be heard almost 2 mi. (3 km) away.

## Finding a Mate

Most of the time, tigers don't meet. They leave spray marks and claw marks on trees to warn others away from their territory. Sometimes, these marks attract other tigers that are looking for a mate or a territory.

Females are ready to mate when they are three years old, and males when they are four. As well as scent-marking and claw-marking, females roar loudly to attract males to mate with. When the female has mated, the cycle of life is ready to begin again. In just over three months' time, the tigress will give birth to cubs of her own.

▼ A female uses her claws to scratch marks on a tree in her territory.

# Threats

Today there are only between 6,000 and 7,000 tigers left in the entire world, half of them in India. Yet, about a hundred years ago there were nearly 50,000 tigers in India alone. The population fell because tens of thousands of tigers were hunted and killed for sport. Many other tigers were badly injured.

▼ Indian soldiers and villagers hold up a tiger skin taken from poachers.

## TIGER HUNTING

Tiger hunting was a popular sport among the British people who governed India until 1947, and the Maharajas, or kings, who ruled parts of the country. Eight to ten tigers might be killed in a single day's shoot.

●

The record for the number of tigers killed was held by the Maharaja of Surguja, who killed 1,100 tigers during his lifetime.

▲ A scientist attaches a radio collar to a drugged tiger so that the tiger's movements can be followed.

To prevent this bloodshed, tiger shooting was banned in India in 1969. Then, in 1972, it was estimated that there were only 1,800 tigers left alive in India. The following year, the Indian government started "Project Tiger," a special project to save the last remaining tigers.

## The Disappearing Forests

India has a huge population, which grows even bigger every year. To make room for all these people, more and more of the tigers' forest home is being cut down.

Sometimes people kill the forest animals that tigers need for food. Then the tigers have to kill animals that belong to villagers who live near the forest. The villagers may then try to kill the tigers with poison.

▼ People cut down forests so they can use the land. These miners, in India, are building homes on land that has been cleared.

► These medicines, made from parts of dead tigers, are sold mainly in China, Taiwan, and Korea.

## Tiger Poaching

Poachers go into the forests to kill the tigers. They lay traps and snares on the forest paths. As a tiger walks along, its leg is caught by the trap. The tiger shrieks in pain, and the poachers who set the trap kill it.

Poachers kill tigers to make money. Tiger skins are seen as trophies, and some people use them as rugs in their homes. Tiger bones are made into medicines because some people in Asia believe they can cure illnesses. Tiger teeth and claws are made into necklaces because people believe these will make them strong. Other parts of the tiger are cooked and eaten as food.

## The Tiger's Future

The world loses more than 400 tigers every year. If this continues, by 2010 there will be hardly any left. Can the tiger survive? The answer will depend on what we can all do to help solve the problems it faces. We must try to make sure that some land is set aside for the tiger and its habitat. By saving tigers, we also save the forests and the animals, birds, insects, and plants that live there.

▲ These schoolchildren in India are performing a play about forests and the animals that live there.

Wildlife protection organizations are working hard to save the tiger. They try to persuade governments to do more to protect their tigers by setting up preserves and national parks and by stopping poachers. They also teach people about the importance of tigers and the forests where they live. You could help by joining or supporting one of these organizations. There is a list of addresses on page 47.

▼ An antipoaching patrol. These men try to stop poachers from killing tigers.

# Tiger Life Cycle

 **1** From one to seven cubs are born about fourteen weeks after the tigress mates with a male tiger. The cubs feed on their mother's milk. Their eyes open between three and fourteen days old.

 **2** During their second month, the cubs start eating meat that their mother hunts. Gradually, the cubs stop drinking milk altogether, and their diet becomes mainly meat.

 **3** When they are five months old, the tigress begins to teach the cubs about the habitat in which they live. At seven months, they go everywhere with her.

**4** From about eight months to twenty months, the tigress teaches her cubs how to hunt, what prey to catch, and where to find it.

**5** At around sixteen months, the cubs start to be less friendly toward each other, and one dominant cub prepares to leave home. By twenty-four months, all the cubs have left their mother.

**6** Females are ready to have their first litter soon after they are three years old. Males tend to be ready to mate after four years. At five years old, they enter their prime. In the wild, tigers can live to between twelve and sixteen years old.

# Glossary

**Antiseptic** Something that kills germs, especially those that cause diseases.

**Camouflage** Colors or patterns that help an animal blend with its surroundings.

**Canine teeth** Long, pointed teeth toward the front of the tiger's jaws. There are two in the top jaw and two in the bottom jaw.

**Carcass** The dead body of an animal, especially one that has been killed for food.

**Dominant** A word describing the strongest and most confident cub in a litter.

**Fertility** The ability of an animal to have young or of land to produce crops.

**Groom** To clean. Tigers groom themselves by licking their fur.

**Guardian** A person or animal that looks after something and keeps it safe.

**Intruder** Someone or something that enters a place where it is not wanted or has not been invited.

**Poachers** People who hunt and kill animals illegally.

**Prey** An animal that is killed by another animal for food.

**Scavenge** To feed on the kill of another animal.

**Scent** A smell left by an animal.

**Stalk** To creep up on something slowly and quietly.

**Suckling** Giving or taking milk from the mother's teats.

**Territory** The area that is controlled and defended by an animal.

**Weaned** Cut off from drinking mother's milk and trained to move on to other foods.

# Further Information

## Organizations to Contact

Care for the Wild International
1 Ashfolds, Horsham Road,
Rusper, West Sussex RH12 4QX
Tel: 01293 871596
Web site:
www.careforthewild.org.uk

Earth Living Foundation
P.O. Box 188
Hesperus, CO 81326
(970) 385-5500

Friends of the Earth
1025 Vermont Avenue NW
Suite 300
Washington, D.C. 20005-6303
(202) 783-7400

Survival International
11–15 Emerald Street
London WC1N 3QL
Tel: 0171 242 1441

World Wildlife Fund
1250 24th Street NW
P.O. Box 96555
Washington, D.C. 20077-7795

## Web Sites

The Tiger Information Center
www.5tigers.org
A site with information and
news about tigers, including
pages especially for children
and with links to other sites.

David Rose's Tiger Page
www.navigator.co.uk/rosie/tiger
Information about tiger species,
extinctions and links to a few
other sites.

## Books to Read

Bailey, Jill. *Save the Tiger* (Earth's Endangered Species). Austin, TX:
Raintree Steck-Vaughn, 1990.

Harris, Amanda. *Tigers* (Endangered). Tarrytown, NY: Benchmark
Books, 1996.

Higgins, Maria. *Cats! From Tigers to Tabbies* (Animal Planet). New
York: Crown Publishers, 1998.

Lumpkin, Susan. *Big Cats* (Great Creatures of the World). New
York: Facts on File, 1993.

Pollack, Steve. *The Atlas of Endangered Animals* (Environmental
Atlas). New York: Facts on File, 1993.

# Index

All the numbers in **bold** refer to photographs or illustrations.

birth 8, 10
buffalo **23**, **27**

claws 4, 33, **37**, 41
coat **4**, **7**
cubs 8, **10**, **11**, 12, **13**, **14**, **15**, 16, 17, **17**, **18**, 19, **19**, **20**, **21**, 24, 29, **30**, 31, 32, **33**, 37, **44**, **45**

dens 8, **9**, **10**, 11, 12, 19

eyes **5**, 10, 44

food **12**, 15, 20, **21**, **23**, 29, 30, 34, 40
forest 4, 19, 23, 27, **40**, 41 42, **43**
fur **7**, 10

leopards 17

monkeys **26**, 27

peacocks 14, **23**, 24
play 14, **18**, 19, **19**, 29

poachers 38, 41, 43
porcupines **23**, 27
prey 4, 20, **22**, **23**, **24**, 31, **45**

rhinos **28**

sambar deer **19**, **23**, 24
sloth bears **23**, **29**

teeth **5**, 11, 23, 30, **36**, 41
territory 13, 20, 30, 31, 32, 34, **37**